# Sales Team Management in a week

ANDREA NEWTON

Hodder & Stoughton

A MEMBER OF THE HODDER HEADLINE GROUP

Orders: please contact Bookpoint Ltd, 130 Milton Park, Abingdon, Oxon OX14 4SB.
Telephone: (44) 01235 827720. Fax: (44) 01235 400454. Lines are open from 9.00–6.00, Monday to Saturday, with a 24 hour message answering service.
Email address: orders@bookpoint.co.uk

*British Library Cataloguing in Publication Data*
A catalogue record for this title is available from The British Library

ISBN 0 340 857951

| | |
|---|---|
| First published | 2002 |
| Impression number | 10 9 8 7 6 5 4 3 2 1 |
| Year | 2007 2006 2005 2004 2003 2002 |



Typeset by SX Composing DTP, Rayleigh, Essex.
Printed in Great Britain for Hodder & Stoughton Educational, a division of Hodder Headline Plc, 338 Euston Road, London NW1 3BH by
Cox & Wyman Ltd, Reading, Berkshire.

# CONTENTS

# Your role and responsibilities

Welcome to our first day together! Over the coming week we will explore what makes a successful sales manager, and provide you with some useful tips and ideas. Perhaps you have recently become a sales manager for the first time, or you have aspirations to move in that direction? Maybe you are already an established sales manager and are looking to refresh your skills? From time to time we will ask you to stop and think about your own situation, and perhaps make a few notes to clarify things for yourself.

Whether you choose to dip in and out of this book or read it from cover to cover, we hope it will give you a clear idea of the role and responsibilities of a successful sales manager. Whatever your situation or preference for using this book, we hope you enjoy your week with us!

## Success or failure?

What makes a successful sales manager? What is it that sets the successful apart from the 'also ran'? Let's look first at a sales manager's primary role and their responsibility to their team, their organisation and themselves.

Whatever your situation, the most important things to come to terms with are your role and responsibilities. A challenge that people face when they become managers for the first time, of any discipline, is to let go of the responsibility of 'doing the job'. Managing a successful team or department is not about hands-on 'doing'. It is a whole new ball game requiring different rules and skills.

Take a moment to think about what you think your responsibilities are.

It is certainly up to you to make sure that sales are won, business is increased, satisfied clients come back for more, and that sales goals and targets are achieved. However, it is not up to you to win the business yourself! That is the role of your team. Your role is simply to help them do that. Sound easy?

It can be difficult to recognise that sales success should not be coming directly from you. Working out in the field and calling on customers are the responsibilities of your team now. Your responsibility, as a manager, is to achieve success through others. Your role is to support your team, motivate them and provide the resources that they need to win business. A useful definition of a manager's role is, 'The Manager must achieve agreed performance objectives and increase overall profit through the members of the team, in an efficient and effective manner'.

If you find yourself calling on customers, to make sure that targets are met and business is won, you are not doing your job as sales manager. So often, newly promoted managers find it hard to separate themselves from the day-to-day activity of winning business, and concentrating on helping their team to do that. Your job is to recruit the right people, put them in the right place, agree goals, support the achievement of those goals and develop their skills so that they can keep on being successful. Your success comes from *their* success, not from selling to clients!

Of course, you may get involved in calls to clients with your team, but again, your role will be a different one. You will be there either to support their efforts, to build a key account by building a relationship with the organisation, or to coach your team out in the field.

Moving to a sales manager role can be a difficult process, and needs commitment and persistence. It also requires un-learning many of the habits you had as an effective salesperson. Traits and behaviours that were useful then, will actually get in the way now, if you are to be a manager in the true sense of the word. Sales management requires a whole new mind-set. Every day you will make decisions that affect your team, your clients and your organisation, and of course, yourself.

- Where are you operating from now?
- Do you think like a salesperson, or like a sales manager?

Sun Tzu, a military strategist in 500 BC wrote in *The Art of War* that: 'Your strengths will eventually become a weakness'! For a salesperson moving to a management role, this can be the case. While your focus was to develop accounts and clients business, it now needs to develop the team. Instead of your own achievements of targets and generating business, you should concentrate on developing and supporting others to do that. Your ability to be self-sufficient and get on with the job as a salesperson has to adapt. You need to learn to delegate and let others do it.

Whereas the role of the sales person is to look for immediate wins, as a manager you should look for longer term gain, which involves a lot of patience, planning and strategic practice. You have to slow down, take a step back and remove yourself from the front line. You are no longer charged with winning business, but with building and maintaining a winning team.

It can hard to make the transition and, to be honest, some people realise that management is not for them. If they made excellent salespeople, it does not mean they will make excellent sales managers. In fact, if being excellent at selling, enjoying the chase, the cut and thrust and the buzz when the client says 'Yes' drove you to succeed, can you settle for more of a back seat, getting the buzz from others taking the driving seat?

## Case study

Another factor that can hinder the transition to sales manager is the culture and attitude of the company you work for. We recently worked with a team of sales managers who simply were not ready to let go and become managers. They kept a lion's share of their team target as their own personal target, and kept a list of clients as their own. As a result they became stressed and very busy, always fighting for time, and always in demand by people who needed their support. They were ineffective as managers because they were not available for their team. They created a dependency that they enjoyed and were proud of. Why did they do this?

By keeping their own targets and winning their own business, the sales managers were protecting themselves. Their organisation valued income-generators, people who brought in revenue – the sales team. The sales figures were the focus of management meetings; the managing director always enquired what new business had been won, and the salespeople were the highest paid. One of the organisation's competitors had been bought out, and the level of management responsible for the sales teams was 'not required' by the new parent company. As a result these sales managers viewed the role of the sales manager as a vulnerable one. It did not generate income, it was not offered incentives and reward, and it was seen as 'easy to get rid of'.

Human instinct determined the need to protect themselves. They felt valued and safe as individuals who brought in the money. The organisation did not seem to recognise the value and benefit of having effective managers who could develop, nurture and grow the team; they valued revenue in the bank. Until the mind-set and culture of the organisation changed, there was no incentive for the sales managers to change their mind-set and see their value in a different way.

A lesson to be learned from this is to clarify and agree your role and value as an effective sales manager. Look at how you are measured and rewarded. Confirm with your senior management team their expectations of you, both in the short and longer term. If the culture does not encourage the change in mind-set required to be an effective manager, the transition you need to make will be even more difficult.

## What makes an effective manager?

After all is said and done, what is it that makes an effective manager? Spend a moment or two thinking about managers that you have worked for. What was it about them that made them a 'good' manager or a 'not so good' manager?

Chances are, the good managers will have listened and welcomed your ideas, involved you in the decision-making process, recognised your achievements and motivated you to achieve more. They probably also made things happen, followed through on promises and supported you in your development and acquisition of new skills. Perhaps they gave you responsibility and did not tell you what to do, how to do it or when to do it – unless it was something new and you asked them for advice. They made the best use of resources, and made sure that whatever was lacking was provided where possible. They communicated clearly and promptly, treated you like an adult, an individual, who was informed and aware of what was required and expected.

You might also describe good managers as fair, honest, open, supportive, encouraging, motivational, reliable, consistent, flexible and understanding. Possibly they had good technical knowledge, were charismatic and adapted their behaviour and style of management to suit the individual and the situation.

And the not so good managers? Perhaps they did not have a clear vision, did not plan, could not adapt their style. Maybe they were very bureaucratic, relying on rules and punishment to make things happen, unaware of what was happening for their team. They kept things to themselves, told rather than discussed and agreed and had mood swings so you never knew where you stood with them. And so the list goes on.

As we move into roles as supervisors or managers, without any formal development, we often adopt the approach and style of what we feel our best manager had. We see them as a role model and take on the behaviours they demonstrated – good or bad. In the same way that a child adopts the values, beliefs and behaviours of others around them, as newly promoted managers we take with us how we have seen it done. However, sometimes this is not necessarily the best way to go.

Consider the skills, traits, qualities and characteristics of a good manager, and compare your list to the one below. Start to think about which of these areas you want to develop yourself, in order to be a successful sales manager.

| **A successful manager will** | **Yes/No** |
|---|---|
| Organise and make best use of time | |
| Plan ahead | |
| Identify the root cause of problems | |
| Possess appropriate decision-making skills | |

| | |
|---|---|
| Communicate clearly and often | |
| Listen to others | |
| Appraise performance and give feedback | |
| Know how to motivate themselves and others | |
| Recruit and retain good staff | |
| Delegate effectively | |
| Remain unbiased and objective | |
| Empathise with others | |
| Manage the development of themselves and others | |
| Manage resources effectively | |
| Be motivated and enthused by their team's success | |

## Management competences

In order to do what you are employed to do successfully, there are underpinning management competences that you need to make sure you have.

To create a sales strategy, you need to be able to plan ahead, think clearly and analytically, forecast and monitor performance, and identify problems and solve them. The ability to think clearly and solve problems is not necessarily something we are taught at school. It may not be a natural behaviour for you. It is, however, an essential skill that you need to develop. Many sales managers focus on the issue of the day, rather than focusing on longer term success. By being reactive to problems that arise and taking on a fire-fighting role, they often find that the same issues appear tomorrow, next week and next month.

How good are you at making decisions? Analysing the situation, uncovering the root cause, thinking of the long-term implications of what, right now, feels like a good idea that, typically, we want to implement as soon as possible. Can you separate yourself from the here and now and look further down the road to what that decision might mean in the future – to you, your sales team, the organisation, clients, indeed any stakeholder?

Do you communicate effectively? Do you ask questions without bias, to uncover information and then actively listen to the response? Barriers that get in the way are our need to speak, our mind working on the response we feel is appropriate or the next question we want to ask. Such matters often cloud our listening. Actively listening involves working hard to remove these barriers, not just to hear the words, but to listen and evaluate and only then to respond accordingly. Again competences that were important to you as a salesperson, but which now need to be utilised to get open and honest answers to help you help your team, not to influence the outcome.

Interviewing for staff is more than 'just a quick chat'. How well do you prepare for and structure interviews? Do you employ your communication and analytical thinking skills to make sure you get the best person for the job? How clear are you in determining who the best person for the job really is?

Once you have recruited your team, do you have the necessary skills and mind-set to support and promote their development? Do you understand their needs and can you align them with the needs of the business? Are you committed to that development, and do you make time to effectively appraise performance to aid further development?

Do you have the necessary skills, knowledge and understanding to manage performance and deal with inappropriate behaviours in a way that is helpful and supportive? Is your style of management too critical or judgemental, making rash decisions based on insufficient information? And once you have the right team in place, do you understand how to motivate them, as well as yourself, in order to achieve the success they desire?

## Summary

As you work through the advice offered in this book, you will start to fully appreciate that the role of a sales manager is not an easy one. In fact, the role of any effective manager is not as easy as it might look. Add to that the responsibility for a team of people who are hungry for success, representing your company to the world at large, who are naturally competitive, selling themselves and your company, and without them and the business they generate, the organisation would not be in business. Do you have what it takes to be a successful sales manager and lead a high performing team to their full potential? This book will point you in the right direction, but only you can develop the right mind-set and make it happen – are you ready for the challenge?

# Goals and targets

You are now clear about your role and what you do in terms of leading your sales team, but what is your overall goal? Typically the goal for the sales team is to increase business, but by how much? From which client(s)? Increasing sales of which product or service particularly? What does the profit margin need to be? By when? How does this fit with the big picture at organisational level? That is part of your goal – enabling the team to hit target, the right target, in line with the organisation's target.

## Integrated strategy

You need to understand first of all what the company wants to achieve. Once you are clear on that, your role and goal should be more apparent. For example, if the company are looking to diversify their products or services over the coming year, perhaps your goal is to encourage your team to establish more customers within a certain market sector. If your company's mission is to consolidate and establish themselves firmly with their existing clients first, then your role will be slightly different – to focus your team on maintaining and developing existing accounts.

It is imperative that you understand what your company is trying to achieve at the organisational level. You need to be aware of the vision, the target, and the overall objective that the organisation is working towards, as well as their plans for the future. You need to not only understand your own purpose, but be able to translate that into something meaningful for all members of your team. Your team's goal should fit with the goals of the other departments as well. For example, if the marketing department are focusing their efforts on attracting clients from a specific industry, surely you should be working hand in hand with them to win business from that market? There needs to be consistency across departments, as well as within your own team. There is little point your team continuing to sell and promote a product that the manufacturing department are having trouble sourcing the materials for! Make sure that you are working in synergy with other departments and that you are all working towards the same desired outcomes. All goals and targets for both individuals and departments should be clearly linked to the goals and targets set for the organisation, and these in turn need to be consistent with each other. Make good use of your communication skills and talk to other department heads. An obvious statement? You will be surprised how many managers work in isolation of others!

- Do you know the goal of the organisation?
- Can you translate that into your departmental or team goal?
- Can you further translate that into something meaningful for the individuals concerned?
- Does your team goal fit with the goals of other departments?
- Are the goals clear, up to date and focused?

## Destination

Having a destination in mind helps when reading the map and agreeing the best route. If I don't know where I am heading for, I will not know which way to go, or indeed whether or not I have arrived. Perhaps the message will be that: 'If it doesn't matter where we are going, does it then matter if we actually get there at all?' If I don't know where I am heading, how will I know if I am on schedule or have fallen behind, and therefore, how much I need to do to catch up?

## Case study

Sales people generally understand that their role is to increase sales and win more business. An organisation in the publishing industry recently reviewed the goals and targets of its team to find that, although they were winning business, the business was coming in from many small accounts, which in turn created much administrative effort. Performing credit checks and generating new accounts caused more work for finance and credit control who were constantly chasing a number of small outstanding amounts. The company really wanted to build solid relationships with larger accounts in the longer term, creating more of a partnership with the client. By doing so they would reduce the number of new credit accounts that had to be opened, and hopefully develop ongoing business with these clients, rather than the cost of constantly generating new business from smaller companies. This vision and objective had not been communicated clearly to the sales team, who were still running around their territory chasing after small amounts of business, at a cost to the organisation.

- Are your team clear about what type of customer you want to attract?

Give your sales team a clear destination, help them plan their route, and support them every step of the way, keeping them up to date with changes and amending the route plan accordingly.

## Specify targets

Once your team are clear on the direction, they then need to know how much business they are expected to generate. Surely it is enough for the sales team to know that their role is to generate as much business as they can? However, if they win a new client, who spends £100, will you be happy? It is as much as they could do, and it is new business, so what is the problem? The problem is, it probably will not meet the expected standard or contribute significantly to achievement of the overall aim. It will probably also mean that they are costing you money and not even generating enough business to cover those costs, let alone contributing to the organisation as a whole.

A salesperson needs more. They need to know how much business you want. They need to know what type of business you want. Do you want business to come from new clients or do you want your team to develop existing accounts? When do you want the team to generate new business by?

No doubt you are aware of the acronym SMART when it comes to setting goals.

- S – Specific
- M – Measurable
- A – Achievable
- R – Realistic
- T – Time bound

- How SMART are your goals?

'To generate new business' is not a SMART goal. Let's break it down step by step.

'To generate 30 per cent increase on last year from new clients in a 40-km radius of the office by the end of June.' This is a SMART goal. It tells us *specifically* what is expected, it can be *measured*, it is *achievable* (you need to decide whether a 30 per cent increase is achievable), it is *realistic* and the *time-scale* is fair.

Spending time discussing and agreeing SMART goals is time well spent. As we shall see later, people do what is measured, and you can manage what you measure. People are also more motivated and driven towards achievement if they are clear on their aims, and have a clear understanding of exactly what is expected.

Clarity in setting goals and targets will make a difference. The salesperson out in the field will know where to channel their energy and enthusiasm. They will be clear on the desired outcome, and you will both be clear on what success looks like. The salesperson will also recognise when they are falling behind, and can then work out what they need to do to get ahead again. They will also realise that success is probably not the one client who spends £100!

## Results and activity targets

In making goals measurable, link them to outcomes or results, not necessarily to activity levels. It is very little use setting a target to visit 50 new prospects every quarter, if none of those prospects become clients and no increase in revenue results. What specifically do you want them to achieve? We will look at how they go about achieving it when we consider suitable strategies, but for now concentrate more on the *what* not the *how.*

However, depending on your business and strategy, you may decide it is appropriate to agree some activity targets – especially with newer salespeople who would appreciate some smaller measurements. These measurements might typically be the number of qualified appointments they should make, the decision to ensure efficiency by measuring kilometres per call, their conversion rate of visits to business won, the number of new contacts they should make each week. You may also need to agree activity targets with someone who is not achieving the overall goal – perhaps they do not appreciate what it takes to win that amount of new business? You will then also monitor activity as well as productivity – be careful that one does not distract you from the other.

## Soft and hard objectives

Depending on your circumstances, it is relatively easy to provide a quantitative measurement of sales success, if you are focusing on the amount of revenue, profit or number of accounts of a certain level you expect the team to generate. Hard objectives can be measured easily in terms of outputs, but it is not always so easy to measure qualitative outcomes, such as customer satisfaction, skill development, personal presentation. Such 'soft' objectives are also important to your team, they cover 'the way the job is done', and tend to define the difference between what is acceptable and what is excellent performance. How can you define these softer objectives so that your salespeople recognise what is expected and exactly what constitutes excellent performance? They are equally valuable in determining success and more thought and definition will probably be required to give a clear direction and target. If you cannot measure it in numerical terms, can you at least describe it and set standards?

The goals that you set both for yourself and your team should always be challenging but achievable. If there is no challenge, and the objectives are easy and come naturally, how will that motivate a good keen salesperson? It is like buying a book of puzzles and finding that the answers are filled in already. For a short time, the lack of effort may be enjoyable, you become an order taker rather than a salesperson, but over time the lack of challenge and personal sense of achievement will probably lead to your team becoming complacent, apathetic, and dare we say it, bored! If a pure-bred racehorse is never allowed or encouraged to do more than a quick 5 minute trot around the yard, it is a waste of energy, desire and ability.

## Motivation

On the other hand, if the goals are too challenging and unattainable, the same effect will result. If the salesperson never manages to hit their target and always running behind where they want to be, for how long will they really sustain 100 per cent effort? Goals should be stretching, challenging and developmental in order to harness enthusiasm and desire to achieve them, but if they are unattainable, motivation and desire will probably drop. Then it is a self-fulfilling prophecy: 'It's too much, I haven't hit target' through to 'It's too high, I'll never do it', through to 'Look, there's little point in trying, I'll never do it'. Human beings are largely driven by achievement – whether achievement of recognition, reward or personal satisfaction. We are excited by achievement and the desire to have more. Make sure the goals that you set motivate your team in this way.

- How will you ensure that the goals you agree with your team are motivating?

To do this you need to match the team's experience and capability with their goals, as well as make sure they do not have too many goals. If a salesperson tries to focus on too many targets and goals, chances are they will not be able to put the effort and energy into fully achieving any. Think back to the last time you felt you had too much on your plate. You perhaps had a number of tasks to complete and had to juggle them all. You probably did not do any of them very well – dividing your energy and enthusiasm, not to mention your

capability, in so many directions means that inevitably something has to give. Something has to slip through the cracks. Imagine if you had fewer goals and could focus and concentrate on them. The outcome would probably be quite different, you would probably do a much better job of a much higher quality because you were able to focus and direct your attention.

Salespeople will be more motivated to achieve their goals if they are involved in agreeing them in the first place. Salesperson are aware of their capabilities and the territory they cover. Involve your team in discussing, agreeing and setting SMART goals, in order to allow them to buy into them and take on the challenge.

Also make sure that the salesperson can control achievement of their goal. If they feel that achievement of the goal relies on other external factors, over which they have no control, for example, a change in legislation, then they cannot reasonably be held accountable for non-achievement. If they are to aim for their goal, they need to own it, accept it and control it.

- Are your team motivated by their goals?
- Do they know and understand them?
- Can they control their achievement?

## So what about the numbers?

Given an overall target of say, £100,000 of new business over the next 12 months, is that a case of splitting the total target by the number of salespeople you employ? Will that ensure an achievable and realistic target for the individuals?

It might do, then again it might not. You will need to take into account their level of experience and knowledge, the area or region they work in, the product or service they sell. For example, it may not be realistic to expect newer members of the team to generate the same amount of business as the more experienced. Take into account their region or territory. One salesperson may have an already saturated territory that could not realistically generate the same level of new business as another, just as on the other hand, a brand new territory may need more time to be worked and your organisation become known, before high levels of business can be reasonably expected.

- Do you understand your team's situation and circumstances?
- Do you actively monitor and review, according to the market?

For example, if you set a target to achieve a 50 per cent increase in business and the salesperson is selling into the airline industry, the terrible events of 11 September 2000 will probably have an impact on the achievement of my goal, at least in the short term, and indeed on the business goal the organisation has set itself. It is imperative that goals and targets are reviewed promptly in the face of such changes, and that economic and market factors are taken into account.

Other matters to consider when reviewing and updating goals are the ability of the organisation to provide the product or service they are selling. If production are struggling to meet capacity, and your team are targeted to achieve a further increase in the sale of this product line, how will you deal with that situation? It is important to be aware of the organisational objectives, yet ensure your targets and goals do not cause conflict or additional problems for others. Make sure they are compatible with other departmental objectives, and the salesperson still has control of achievement!

## Sales support

It is your responsibility to ensure that the resources that support the sales process are available. This might be literature, demonstration products, sales support staff based in the office, a reliable car that projects the right image, up-to-date pricing lists and catalogues, a website that is easy to find and use, and whatever other equipment or resources are pertinent to the success of your team. You need to budget for and manage resources, as well as people, if you are to successfully manage a sales team.

Your ability to communicate well at all levels and be aware of what is happening throughout the business, not just with your team, is extremely important. Your team is relying on you to provide the support they need to achieve their goals; you have to keep them up to date and think clearly and analytically about longer term results. Think carefully about factors that could impact or hinder, and in some cases, factors that might see a dramatic upward trend in demand. Be on the look out for such opportunities and be ready to react and guide your team to respond to them – it is amazing how many street vendors appear selling cheap umbrellas when there is a sudden, unexpected heavy downpour of rain! They know their market and are proactive and ready to respond to it.

## Sales cycle

As far as the time factor is concerned, this will need to be agreed according to your own personal circumstances and industry. Also consider the typical sales cycle in your business – how long does it take for a prospect to become a client? Some industries have a short sales cycle, such as office consumables, where clients use these items on a daily basis and are buying regularly. On the other hand, in the technology or heavy machinery industries, where clients may only purchase once every 5 years, where costs are high, or where products themselves have longer lives, the sales cycle is much longer. In the training industry, clients can take anything from a few weeks to a few years to decide to make a purchase. The initial discussions and planning can take a long time, the design will be agreed and, finally, it is hoped, the client will give the go ahead to deliver a bespoke programme. Clients do not tend to invest in training with a new provider at the drop of a hat – they need time to consider, understand, and get to know the trainers, and then the time needs to be right for the implementation of the training to have maximum benefit to the people and the business.

- What is the sales cycle length in your organisation and industry?

You may also need to consider the typical peaks and troughs in business cycles – it may not be realistic to set a high target for Christmas tree sales in July, nor for the increase in ice-cream cones sold in December. Are you aware of seasonal trends in your business? Will the long summer break typical in European countries cause a slow-down in business? Will you continue to make sales to schools of educational products from July to September? Will there be an increase in spend towards the end of the tax year when government offices are using up what is left of their budget? Know your market, as well as your team!

By considering your own sales cycle, the realistic expectation of the individual salesperson according to their circumstance and experience, and the needs of the business, you will agree a fair target with regards to the time factor. Always make sure that there *is* a time factor – people need to know *by when* you expect them to achieve.

## Summary

Make sure that you are measuring the right thing – what gets measured generally gets done, and what gets measured gets managed. Do also consider that typically what gets managed is often what is easy to measure – are you measuring the right thing? Are you setting the right goals? Do they link to business goals and are they compatible with other departments' goals? Most importantly, will achievement of those goals lead to achievement of organisational success? Focus on the goals that will impact most on the achievement of organisational objectives, and remember to personalise goals for individuals. Not only goals for achievement of business, but also goals for personal development. The 'soft' goals can make all the difference!

- Review your own and your team's goals in light of what you have just learned

# Strategy and vision

Knowing your role and being clear on your team's goals is one thing, knowing how to achieve them is another. This is an area worthy of time and attention. Too many sales teams understand *what* they need to achieve, but are at a loss as to *how*.

You will have made some of the 'how' clear in your goal setting. For example, what type of account you want to win, whether the business is to come from existing accounts or new, whether it is a particular product or service that is to be sold. If you are to truly succeed as the manager of a sales team, you need to have a well-defined strategy, and a strategy and vision that is communicated to the team. It needs to be helpful to them in their day-to-day activities.

## The journey

Return to our example of the goal being similar to knowing your final destination on a journey. Well, the strategy is the

road map you will use to help you get there. Developing your route on the map requires you to consider the variables and options available to you. For example, do we want to use the motorway for this journey, or would the scenic 'A' roads be preferable? This could be seen as our sales channels – a large sales force out in the field, or a small office-based telesales unit. Are there any limitations to the options we have? For example, with a 50cc motorcycle the motorways are not an option. Working with a small telesales unit would limit the option of using exhibitions as part of our sales strategy. If we want to get to our destination, is there anything along the way that might stop us? We need to anticipate problems and plan for them. If we are travelling in the winter months, for instance, we might anticipate the risk of snow, and plan a route which will enable us to deviate quickly to the main roads, therefore still achieving our target on time. In the sales world, the snow might be a competitor that is launching a similar product, causing us to re-evaluate our strategy, or indeed it could be a downturn in business due to a seasonal cycle.

## Team involvement

In planning an effective sales strategy that will enable our sales team to achieve their goals and targets, we need a good understanding of the resources available, our marketplace, customers, competitors and organisational aims and plans. We also need to include the team in agreeing the strategy, just as you would discuss and agree the preferred route for the journey with the driver. The team needs to know where they are going and to have input on the best way to get there. After all, they are the ones out there on the road or on the telephone, with probably the most up-to-date knowledge and information of the market and potential problems. They will also be far more likely to buy into and be accepting of the strategy if they have a part in its development. Time and time again, people are more motivated and determined to achieve something if they have been involved in agreeing what it is, and how it will be achieved, and if they can control it, as we discussed on Monday. Set aside some time to discuss the team's ideas and opinions. A high performing team contributes to its own goals and strategy and everyone moves towards the same goal. The team does not go off in different directions, with each individual having their own idea of what the strategy is.

- Take time to work with your team and agree the most appropriate strategy with them

## Planning the strategy

When planning the strategy, we need to look first at the type of clients we are seeking to attract. Not only in terms of their industry sector, but also matters like size, geographical location, spending power and so on. What is our target market? Who are our targeted prospects? Where will we find them?

With regards to the clients themselves, are we planning to achieve our goal through targeting large multinational organisations or are our ideal clients smaller companies who are local to us? What type of account would have most potential?

For example, if you were selling a computer system, is this system more likely to appeal to larger companies with a network requirement, and what potential would there be for 'selling up'? That is, as well as selling the system, would we also be able to sell in peripherals, maintenance contracts, software?

- Identify now who your ideal clients would be
- Their business potential
- Location, size and the type of client
- Be clear on who your ideal client is and why, and help your sales people to identify similar companies to focus their attention on

This is the kind of information you should be including in your strategy for success – not only the destination, but the route by which we are most likely to reach that destination. Having agreed the size and type of clients we are keen to attract – we now just need to find them.

Who are they and where will we find them? We need to establish where we can get the information about such clients so that we can contact them. Knowing what we want does not make them come running to us – success only comes before work in the dictionary!

Do we need *new* prospect information or are we focusing on clients who already do business with us? Should we focus on clients to whom we have sold recently, and perhaps look to further develop that relationship by promoting a wider product range to them? Do we have a sufficient source of information ourselves, perhaps from previous sales efforts, or do we need to generate fresh information and leads?

If we want new information, details about companies we do not already know, perhaps we would look at purchasing a mailing list, depending on our sector, product and budget available. More importantly, can we source a good quality, up-to-date list that will be worthwhile? Many mailing lists can be a waste of time and money because the information is out of date, unreliable and irrelevant to our business needs. However, perhaps you are aware of a good source of such information and have found this to be a useful method in the past.

If we are to purchase such a list, then how will we make best use of it? What method are we going to use to gain interest from our potential clients? Will we create a direct mail campaign, followed up by our sales team or will we simply use the list and have our sales team start to contact them? Think about the likely success rate and the cost versus benefit of working in this way.

There are potential benefits of each of these strategies. What will work best for you will depend on your specific circumstances. Again, concentrate on the strategy that will have most impact on your overall target, and remember, you can change your strategy if it is not working.

We now know who our target market is, but how will the sales team contact them? Will they use the list to make telephone calls to establish the clients' current situation and interest in our product or service, or will we use the list to send a mailshot? Remember that different methods have different success rates. What is going to be the most effective, both in terms of cost and effort?

Alternatively, perhaps our strategy would be to participate in an exhibition aimed at our client market. With this comes the cost and logistics of attending such an event. This will largely be determined by your budget, whether your product is one that lends itself to such a sales strategy, and whether or not you have sufficient sales staff and skills to make the most of what can be a costly affair. You also need to consider the time, cost and resources needed to follow up leads after the exhibition. An exhibition could be a possible way to achieve your targets this year, but is not to be taken on lightly without investigating potential success versus the cost of that success.

You may want to consider advertising as a way to generate potential clients. If you are considering such a marketing channel, you need to carefully think about the most appropriate media for your company, based again on the product, target audience, location and budget. It can be a costly way to promote your business, with a risk of limited returns, and should be in line with the overall strategy of the organisation. Again, it has to be compatible and part of the total business strategy. Think again about the cost, and whether you are able to follow up the response effectively.

## Selling

Once we have decided who we are to contact, and where we will find them, the strategy needs to now focus on *how* we will sell to them. Your specific circumstances – product, budget and sales force – will dictate this.

Bear in mind that selling in today's marketplace is very different from the way it was, say 10 years ago. Nowadays competition is much more fierce and the chances are, whichever market you are in, you are not the only organisation providing that particular product or service. As a result, prices have been driven down in many industries and buyers have become more sophisticated in their practices and behaviours. In today's business world, buyers want to minimise the risk of making the 'wrong' decision, and are more aware, astute and prudent in making sales purchases.

The market has changed and the 'Seven steps to selling' is not enough. Clients want more, expect more, demand more – and doing business has become easier because of the change in technology and availability of information.

When considering your sales strategy, it may be useful to think of other ways of reaching your target market, rather than the traditional routes of advertising, exhibitions, cold calling and mailshots. Your competitors are probably also using these same methods, so the customer may just see you as one of many. As we have already identified, in today's business world, it is unlikely that you will not have many competitors. Perhaps consider how you might stand out from the crowd. How your team can achieve success by being more creative and 'different' in your approach.

As we have also indicated, clients are more prudent in their decisions to buy. What can you do to make potential customers more aware of you, and importantly, more comfortable with the decision to do business with you? What will give your team the edge over others who are selling the same product or service?

In your strategy, you might also consider how your current customers can help you increase business. Perhaps your sales people can ask them for referrals to other colleagues or companies that would have an interest in what you are selling? Asking your satisfied clients for referrals or recommendations could also form an important part of your strategy.

How else can you build up the confidence of a new client to enable them to do business with you? Look for other opportunities of getting in front of them. Are there business clubs, industry events, network meetings where your clients are likely to be in attendance? Perhaps your largest market has a professional Institute, such as the Institute of Logistics, the Chartered Institute of Personnel and Development, and so on. If so, consider the opportunities that membership of such bodies might generate: the opportunity to network with and meet potential clients in a 'non sales' environment. Build up the relationship, without selling to them, in order to increase confidence and awareness of your company and what you can offer. Encourage your team through your strategy to make the most of such opportunities, and think about where you are likely to find potential clients. Get to know them, get your name known and use every opportunity to promote your products and services. Consider also meetings at local Chamber of Commerce or Business Clubs and Networks, and depending on your industry and knowledge, consider being a Guest Speaker on a topic of relevance and interest to the audience. Do more than your competitors and with a planned, strategic approach, the need for cold-calling and mailshots may decrease – now there's a nice thought!

Your strategy might also consider other ways of getting your name and your company's reputation known. Perhaps working with your marketing department, if you have one, to investigate opportunities such as editorial coverage in industry publications. Try a well placed article of an interview with a satisfied customer, sponsorship of an event or free give-aways (if your product lends itself in this way) to delegates at conferences or seminars.

Also consider your website. Today people don't ask 'Do you have a website?', it is more usual to hear 'What's your website address?' Make sure your website is incorporated in your strategy and that it is used to its full potential. If you do not already have an internet presence, perhaps this is something you might consider and take professional advice to see if this is a worthwhile investment for you.

In defining your sales strategy, you need to be a little more creative perhaps than before. Look 'outside the box' for opportunities and include them in a well-defined, focused and meaningful strategy, that ties together all the different strands and really helps your sales people map out their journey to sales success.

## Summary

When considering your strategy for your sales team, you also have to appreciate that today there are far more sales channels available to clients, such as call centres where business is conducted over the telephone, the arrival of the internet and the ability to shop online without the need for a salesperson to call. Due to the decrease in the cost of sales through such channels, you could find you are working in an industry where not only are there more potential suppliers, but where prices are lower and the ways in which you can buy, are more.

In developing the strategy for your team, it is imperative to be aware of the factors that will impact on its success. If your organisation has other sales channels, such as an internet presence where clients can shop online, what should the role of your sales team be? Perhaps they should focus more on developing long-term business by developing a partnership approach with your clients? If the initial sale is made through another channel, should they then be looking at ways of adding value to the relationship, rather than being involved in the creation of it from the outset?

- A strategy is only useful if it helps us to achieve what we want. How effective is your strategy for success?

# Team work

A sales manager cannot be effective unless they know their team. After all, as we have already discussed, the role of the sales manager is to achieve results *through* their people. It is essential that you spend some time with your people both in the office and, if relevant, in the field. You need to not only know them as people, and be aware of their targets and territory, but also recognise their strengths and areas for development.

## Get to know the team

Just as the manager of a football team would identify where the strengths of his team lay when deciding who to put in goal and who should take penalty kicks, you need to know your people to agree the right goals and objectives, and to ensure they are selling the right products and services in the right marketplace. You also have a responsibility to develop their skills and knowledge in order to help them win business successfully. After all, as a manager, their success is your success.

When taking over an established team, the first step would be to analyse the players and their performance, and to familiarise yourself with their area or territory. Take time to get to know your team as individuals, and recognise that each may have their own style of selling – your way is not the only way. With this, you may have to flex your management style to suit each one. We all have our own preferences and behaviours, and a good sales manager will recognise and value this.

- How well do you know *your* team?

Getting to know your people can start as a simple exercise you can do by yourself. For example, draw up a grid and list the names of all your salespeople on the left-hand side. Across the top fill in areas or questions you need to find the answers to, such as territory covered, experience, results, key clients won and so on.

How much do you know about each salesperson? Don't fall into the trap of basing your answers on assumption or on what other people have told you. Successful sales managers find out first-hand about their people, and do not prejudge them. Fill in any information you know already, including a brief outline of your first impression. First impressions are not always lasting ones, but customers will also judge your people out in the field in this way.

From there you can continue by looking at your team's personnel files. See how long they have been with the company, what background they have, what formal development they have had and what their recent success rate has been. You may also have copies of their previous appraisals or performance reviews, and you should also have their targets for previous sales periods and their success rate. All this information should be noted in a methodical manner and will form the basis of your 'Getting to know you' exercise. This will help you to implement your strategy for success.

Incidentally, if such a system is not in place for recording results and achievements, start one immediately! This will help you to plan and review and to forecast and budget. It is imperative that you keep a record of historic data; this will help you to roll out your strategy and review it in the future.

Now go and spend time with your team on the field. You might want to first introduce this idea by bringing them all together and communicating with them as a team. Use this as an opportunity to introduce yourself to them and explain your reason for wanting to spend time with them. Emphasise your desire to get to know them and support them in their role. Setting the scene in this way, in an open and honest manner, can go a long way to developing your relationship with them. Perhaps make this an item for the Sales Meeting agenda – discuss what you would like to get from the visit, and ask the team to suggest what would be useful for them?

An informal meeting like this will also give the team an opportunity to find out about you, ask any questions they might have, and maybe even set their mind at rest as to who you are and find out what you are like. After all, if you were appointed to a new manager, wouldn't you want to know about them?

You then may decide to have a one-to-one meeting with each team member. Find out a little more about them, their territory, any specialist knowledge or skills they might have, how their products and services are selling at the moment and their overall current situation. This will start to give you a better understanding of how they work and where they work (if field-based), as well as a feel for how they are doing in the current sales period. Their responses will also give you an indication of morale – how motivated and enthusiastic they are. Even if they have the skills and knowledge, without motivation they may not be doing your company justice in the marketplace. Now agree an appropriate time and place to join them and see them in action.

## Out in the field

Make sure you emphasise to the salespeople the purpose of this visit; you are not there to catch them out, simply to learn more about them and their situation so that you can do your best to support them in their role. You might want to suggest that they arrange meetings with new as well as existing clients, for you can see them at work in both cases, rather than just seeing how well they get on with clients they know.

- This visit is a fact-finding mission
- Learn as much as you can about the salesperson and their role, their ability and any training needs
- Start to get a feel for any concerns they have or barriers they need to overcome
- Make the day as informal and relaxed as you can, build rapport

Prepare yourself for this field visit by making a note of all the areas you want to look at. For example, a simple check-list of their sales process could be along the lines of:

- Their appearance and approach to clients
- Their ability to build rapport quickly and adapt to the customer's style
- Their ability to open the call and clarify the customer's needs
- Their ability to present the relevant benefits of your product or service
- Their ability to deal with any objections and negotiate effectively
- Their ability to close the call

You may choose to develop this check-list further for future reference. An example might be:

| **Sales Person:** | **Territory:** | | | | | **Date:** |
|---|---|---|---|---|---|---|
| | 1 | 2 | 3 | 4 | 5 | Comments/ feedback |
| Rapport/approach – flexibility | | | | | | |
| Clarifying needs – questioning skills | | | | | | |

| | | | | | | |
|---|---|---|---|---|---|---|
| Presentation skills | | | | | | |
| Objection handling | | | | | | |
| Product knowledge | | | | | | |
| Closing | | | | | | |
| Negotiation | | | | | | |
| Time and territory management | | | | | | |
| Attitude | | | | | | |
| Personal presentation | | | | | | |

This will give you an easy to use structure when sitting in on calls. You can then use this format as the foundation for an assessment check-list when you conduct field visits in the future. This will allow you to identify training needs.

When using any sort of check-list or observation sheet, consider involving your team in its initial design and preparation. Asking the salespeople to contribute to its design, will help it to seem less threatening and more familiar. It is only fair that if you are to use this to assess their performance in future, they understand what is involved.

If you involve your team at this early stage, you can use it as an opportunity to explain what you feel are the important skills for success in their role. In this way, they will know and understand what is important to you as their manager. By consulting them, you can also hear their views on essential skills and gain a better appreciation of their style and opinions.

- What skills or competences will you need to measure with your sales people?
- How will you involve them in the design?
- What further benefits can you gain by involving them in such a way?

## On the day

When observing the team on calls, remind them of the purpose of your visit and take time at the start of the day to build rapport and ease their concerns. Let's face it, regardless of how well we have set the scene previously, there might still be a degree of suspicion and anxiety. Unfortunately salespeople do not always perceive accompanied visits as valuable and motivating and much of this is down to the attitude of the sales manager. Opening the day with a statement like 'So let's see if you're as good as you say you are' will do nobody any favours!

During the calls themselves, resist any temptation to get involved or to jump in to save the sale if you think they are losing it. Take a back seat and observe and note performance issues. You can then take these up after the event and help the salesperson to develop and fine-tune essential sales skills. This will be a far better use of your time and reap rewards in the long term. We will look at dealing with performance issues and training of staff on Thursday.

Physically, it might be a good idea to position yourself to the side and slightly behind your sales representative in client calls. That way you are far less likely to get involved in the actual sales process. Keep your mouth shut and your eyes and ears open!

Remember, your role is to enable the salesperson to generate business. In addition to considering their sales ability, think about whether they also have the right resources to support the sales process. Contemplate the resources we discussed earlier and use this opportunity to get the salesperson's point of view. This investment of your time will help you to build a clear picture of your team, their current situation, and assess whether the right support is in place to meet the targets you have agreed.

You should plan to conduct field-based assessments on a regular basis, and not only with new members of the team. Even the more experienced should be accompanied – quite often familiarity within a role can lead to complacency, and complacent salespeople do not win business! Establish this as part of your performance management process and, from it, you can identify areas that need addressing, as well as using the time to motivate and manage your team.

## Summary

Now you can begin to review the situation.

- Have you got the right people in place?
- Do they have the necessary skills, and if not, can they be trained?
- If they cannot be trained, how will you handle it?
- Is the current sales strategy working in the marketplace?
- What information have you gleaned that will help you to develop or amend your strategy?

Remember to follow up any issues or concerns the team might raise with you during this process. They need to know they can rely on you to see things through. It is no good uncovering problems or concerns and then doing nothing about it – do what you said you would do!

You may want to hold off storming in with new ideas and ways of changing what the team currently do – find out first, understand their situation and learn from them. Only afterwards, once you have had a chance to review and reflect on your findings, can you really start to identify what now needs to happen. Be open to the sales force's suggestions and ideas, and listen, really listen, to their concerns and criticisms – nobody likes a know-it-all.

The way you establish yourself within the first few months of taking on this role will count towards your future success. Do not expect to just pick up the reins and take over where someone else left off. Take some time to really get to know the situation, and the people you are now responsible for supporting, managing, developing and motivating. As Stephen Covey says, 'Seek first to understand, then to be understood'.

The question of whether or not you have the right people, is *not* one you can answer on this first round of accompanied visits. These visits may raise warning signals for you, which should be monitored, but be careful not to jump to hasty conclusions about staff. Wait until you have taken some more time to thoroughly understand them and their situation. Make sure that people have had every opening and the support to develop skills they are lacking. Check that you appreciate their situation and any constraints they might have on them.

There comes a point where you need to be quite analytical and decide: 'Are they trainable? Is there anything more we can do to support them?' Alternatively, you may find that they are holding your team back; they are a liability and no amount of training will rectify the situation. Take time to consider every possible angle, but accept that you may not have the right people in place to turn your strategy into business success. You are responsible for managing their performance, and we will consider how you deal with that tomorrow.

- What can you do to enable you to know your people and their role?
- How do you plan to improve on this?

## Summary

Knowing your team and the individual players within it is critical to success. These are the people who will produce the results you desire. These are the people you rely on for your own success, so make sure that you know who they are and what their strengths, areas for development, and preferences are.

Make sure the team has all the necessary resources and support to enable it to succeed – a team is only as strong as its weakest link. Excellent effort and motivation out in the field will have no impact on sales results if the support behind the scenes is lacking. If, for example, you have telesales staff supporting the activity, then it goes without saying that you need to be just as familiar with their strengths and abilities as you are with your field-based team. Make sure that you are familiar with everyone involved in the sales process and that they are all working to the same standards and goals.

If you really want to lead a successful sales team, you will need to recognise each individual for who they are, and be prepared to communicate, support and interact with them to get the best out of them. Just as a sales person has to adapt behaviour and approach with different clients, a sales manager needs to do the same with the players in her team. A high performing team has a common goal, is supportive of each other and has a leader who inspires, motivates and co-ordinates success. You can't do that until you adapt your own approach to suit this ideal. One size does not fit all – one management style will not have the same effect on all the players.

# Performance management

Everything a sales manager does should focus on helping their team to succeed. The area of training and development is of critical importance to achieve this. Starting from the day a new recruit joins your organisation and throughout their career with you, investing in the development of sales skills should generate a positive return if handled well.

## Induction

An applicant has been chosen and a start date agreed. Put yourself in their shoes. If you were joining a new organisation in a sales role, what would you want to get out of your first day?

They will need to assimilate product and company knowledge very quickly and thoroughly. They will need to understand the process for placing an order through to delivery of the goods or services. What authority do they have to discount the prices in order to win business? What credit period can they offer? What other factors can they use to negotiate with a client? How will you make sure your new recruit has the answer to these, and other potentially challenging questions?

Plan review stages throughout the induction period, and perhaps build in a role-play scenario with you as the customer. This will help to uncover any gaps in the salesperson's knowledge. You may also want to accompany them on first visits to clients, just to ensure they are comfortable and knowledgeable, and representing your company in the best way.

Please do not make the mistake of meeting the new salesperson at 9 a.m. on day one, giving them a quick tour of the building, briefly introducing them to other staff, and then handing them a telephone and directory and expecting them to get on with it. How effective do you *really* think they are likely to be at this point, and what message would that convey to them about you?

Make sure that you are there to welcome the new recruit on their first day. Make sure that you introduce them to all other members of staff. Give them the opportunity to see what happens within your organisation, to ask questions and to learn from the experience. It is not uncommon for new recruits to leave at the end of day one never to be seen again, if their induction has consisted of being left to fend for themselves. Plan the agenda in advance, be there to supervise their first day, and perhaps appoint a mentor for them who will offer additional support during the early days.

- How effective is your induction process?

## Ongoing support

As you become more familiar with your team, and they with you, start to build in regular performance assessment by repeating the assessment check-list exercise, perhaps on a monthly or quarterly basis, depending on the size of your team and territory. During field visits you will have the opportunity to observe, assess, coach, develop and motivate your staff – use the time well. Make sure they focus on the goals you have agreed, and if not, find out *why* not.

With regular appraisal and review, you will be able to quickly identify any problems or development needs your people might have. How you then meet these development needs is very much down to personal skill, preference and budget.

You might feel that you are capable of dealing with the training issues yourself, or perhaps you have an in-house trainer. Alternatively, you may choose to enlist the help of an external consultant who can work more effectively with your team. It is important to be clear about what you are trying to achieve and what gaps need filling. Take into account desired performance and compare that to current performance. What needs to happen for current to meet desired? Training may not always be the answer, and being a trainer is not as easy as it looks, so always consider your options carefully.

## Case study

You are responsible for a team of 12 sales representatives. Eight of these are performing well and meeting monthly targets, consistently. Four of them, all based in the South East, are struggling to meet target. When you go out to assess these four in the field on accompanied visits, you find they are really struggling to sell against a new local competitor who has recently come into the marketplace. The competitor is selling a very similar service, but undercutting your pricing by 30 per cent every time. They can afford to do this because they are selling the service as a loss leader, to enable them to get a foothold in the marketplace.

- What would you do to help your sales people maintain and win business?

## Training issues

You might say that, in this situation, training will not solve the problem, and generally, you could be right. What if you focus on the negotiation part of the sales process, and develop the salespeople's skills in this area? Perhaps concentrate their efforts on trading of concessions and away from discounting of price. Or get the team to focus on what they could offer to the customer that would be perceived as high value and could command your higher price.

Be aware that training is not a panacea. It will not address every performance issue. Further developing your sales team's skills in selling benefits and overcoming objections cannot help their business, if the problem is that the customer is constantly let down by poor service from your after-sales team. Be careful not to see training as the solution to all problems, and be prepared to take time to investigate further, using your clear and analytical thinking skills.

However, if training is the solution, how will it be delivered? Consider whether you have the skills to train – being able to do something well does not necessarily mean you also have the skill to train or teach someone else to do it. If you do, perhaps one-to-one coaching and practice might be useful – role-playing, feedback, discussion. Or perhaps a group session is more beneficial?

## Coaching

Whether you choose to develop your skills as a trainer is a personal choice, but as a sales manager you should definitely look at your ability to coach your team.

A good coach meets regularly with his players and focuses on a specific behaviour or skill to improve. You will need to go out with your salespeople on a regular basis and see them at work. Agree with them an area they would benefit from working on for each meeting, and concentrate solely on that. Coaching sessions are all about helping people to develop, they are not about performance reviews or disciplinary matters.

Cultivate the habit of coaching your people. Ask them to tell you how they could improve their behaviour. Do not simply rely on telling them what they need to do and how they need to do it – coaching is about encouraging the salesperson to think it through for him or herself and to apply appropriate actions.

To be skilled as a coach, you need to develop your ability to question, guide and support – not question, tell, correct and coerce! Salespeople who have had the benefit of a good coach consistently achieve good results, and are motivated and enthusiastic about doing so.

- Do you have the necessary skills and qualities to enable you to support your team in this way?

A popular and simple model you might want to refer to while developing this coaching relationship is the GROW technique. (Adapted from *Coaching for Performance. A Practical Guide to Growing your Own Skills*, Nicholas Brealey, 1993). This comes from a sports coaching scenario, but is equally applicable here.

GROW stands for:

- **G**oal – what do you want to achieve?
- **R**eality – what situation is the salesperson operating in?
- **O**ptions – how might they improve this skill?
- **W**ill – do they have the desire to make it happen?

A good coach does not need to be the best player. A good coach will have experience and knowledge of the task themselves, but their main attribute is to be able to help the

player to focus on specific skills and, through excellent questioning skills, be able to help them concentrate on improvement. Excellent communication and supporting skills are far more important than whether you personally scored all the goals at Wembley! The ability to encourage others to articulate the situation and options for themselves is far more useful than just telling people how to do it. That is what coaching is about.

To be a good coach involves first of all observing your team in action. Remember not to get involved in the call itself, but take a back seat and note what is happening. Use the opportunity to gain insight into what works well and areas that would benefit from improvement. Sales people often spend so much time working on their own that they get into habits, not always good ones, and it can be really helpful to have some feedback and the opportunity to step off the wheel and take time out to review their own performance. This review will be even more powerful if supported by a positive manager.

A good process for coaching has several stages. The following steps will serve as a possible framework for you:

- Immediately after the call, get *their* feedback first – do not jump in with yours straight away
- Ask questions in a supportive and constructive manner so that the salesperson can review and analyse their own performance first
- If you can help them to think about it themselves and have them make suggestions for improvement, they will be more willing and committed to the changes required to improve performance

- Ask questions like, 'What was your objective for the call?', and really listen to the answers. From there you can lead them to consider whether this was fully achieved
- Ask questions like, 'What did you do well?' and in doing so find the positives and reinforce them first
- Once this has been covered you could then go on to ask, 'What might you have done differently?'
- Do NOT ask, 'What was wrong with the call?' This type of question will only cause them to put up their defences and close their mind to the possibilities.

Careful and skilful questioning, done in the right manner, will enable the individual to really review the process and learn from it. You might then lead on to other areas, and agree where to concentrate first. Do not attempt to change too many things at once – habits are hard enough to break without aiming for the impossible of everything at once. Once you have agreed the priority, focus only on that. Draw up an action plan to imrove their skill in this area, and then both commit to it. You might want to demonstrate alternative options they could try, ask them to suggest ideas, and agree the most appropriate course of action. Remember that everyone has their own style of selling – yours is not necessarily the only or best way!

Coaching does not end there. There needs to be repetition and reinforcement of the learning and opportunities to practice and persevere. Coaching is a long-term process, not a one off event, so you need to be patient and persistent and support their efforts and attempts. Encouragement and empathy will be your greatest allies throughout this process.

Through your interaction with them, the sales person needs to understand you are there to help them achieve their full potential, and not as a threat, to judge, criticise and condemn! Only then will they have the commitment and desire to change their actions. Remember, habits are hard to break. Would you be most likely to succeed if your 'coach' kept saying to you 'I thought you were going to stop doing that?' Surely you would be far more likely to persevere and implement the new behaviour if you had positive encouragement and praise of your efforts?

If you can develop your skills as a coach, in order to help your team develop, the outcome can only be win-win. They become more skilled and competent, and with that more confident, and you perform your crucial role of helping your team to succeed. What else can you do to help your team develop and improve? Remember, their success is your success.

You might also consider helping the salesperson to develop skills by role playing typical scenarios with them. Again, centre on one area at a time. You could appoint mentors for the less-experienced person, if you feel you have successful members of the team with the skill and time to support others. This can be an especially useful tack if you have a large team and cannot physically support them all as much as you might like to.

- Look for openings where you can help your people to develop

In addition to accompanying them on the job, you might

organise training sessions for the team, or indeed incorporate a development session into your sales meetings. We will look at that idea again on Saturday.

## Managing performance

A good performance management system is easy to implement and conduct. It does not involve completing reams of paperwork, nor is it a cumbersome millstone around your neck, driven by the human resources department. It is a living document, referred to often and considered almost like a map. If you follow it, it will lead you to your desired destination! Some guidelines to follow are suggested below:

- Agree with each individual their specific role and perhaps four or five key performance indicators as their personal target
- Make targets SMART (Specific, Measurable, Achievable, Realistic and Timed)
- Agree any training or support needed to achieve personal targets
- Agree a review date to assess progress and achievement

*Example*

For a field salesperson, you might agree the following four key indicators:

- Achieve *new* sales revenue target of £100K by the end of March

- Submit weekly report in line with company procedure by 10 a.m. Monday morning
- Develop existing business in all areas by average 5 per cent spend per account by the end of March
- Reduce kilometres per call to an acceptable level of 25 by the end of March

Then, at the end of March, you should agree a time and place to review their achievements. By agreeing SMART targets, you should be able to assess immediately whether or not they have been achieved, and remove the risk of any grey areas as much as possible.

You may choose to incorporate the salesperson's annual or quarterly target, whichever is most appropriate for your business, and any other matters relevant to their success as a salesperson in your organisation, depending on the agreed goals.

You can then discuss with the salesperson, at the end of each review period, their achievements. Agree new achievements for the next review period, taking into account any training needs that have become apparent. Consistent non-achievement of target may result in disciplinary action being taken, assuming that the promised support has been forthcoming, and this should be made clear to them.

At this point, you should refer to your human resources department for guidance, if you have one. If not, consult with someone who understands employment law and can advise you appropriately. Bear in mind that you need to allow a fair and reasonable time for targets to be met, but on the other hand, delaying disciplinary action is unfair to your team and your organisation. Your role is to win business through managing your team, and you might have to face the reality of letting a member of the team go.

## Follow-up action

First things first – did the salesperson know and understand what they were expected to achieve? Did they have the necessary tools, resources, training and time to do so? Perhaps now you need to really think about whether this person is trainable? Can they change their behaviour? Is there anything more that the organisation can do to help them? If the answer to this is no, you may have to take action towards helping the salesperson to move on to something more suitable, and remove the weakest link of your team. In today's competitive marketplace, where people do make the difference, you need to be sure you have the right people in your team. However, what if you have unsuitable staff?

It cannot be stressed enough – make sure that you adhere to your organisation's policy and procedure in such circumstances. There are guidelines and legislation, which pertain to how situations should be handled. Be clear on what they are.

The first stage is normally to have a formal discussion and to issue the individual with a verbal warning, with a review date agreed. Unsatisfactory results at the review date will then lead to a formal, written warning and, further down the line, dismissal may be imminent. This procedure requires time, patience and continued support for the individual. Once issued with a warning, it is not uncommon to be handed the salesperson's resignation soon afterwards. The salesperson recognises that the time has come to move on and tends to do so quite quickly. Something to think about when recruiting is whether you are getting someone else's salesperson who is 'jumping ship before they are pushed?' It is essential to always check out references at interviews.

## Summary

It can be very frustrating to have a salesperson who is not making enough appointments, generating enough business or spending much of their time 'out of contact'. They are costing you money, wasting your time and impacting on the overall results of your team.

A well-designed and well-used performance management system will help you to spot these problems early and to rectify them. If someone is not making the grade, try to make this process as painless and quick as possible – asking salespeople to work their one month notice period can be damaging for your company, clients and other sales staff.

- Do bear in mind that there are steps to follow, both with regard to legislation and with regard to your commitment to managing in a fair and supportive manner.
- Don't drag your feet and hope that a problem will fix itself or go away
- If you do not have the right players in your team, with the right skills and desire, then either help them up or help them out

# Recruitment and selection

At some point you may find yourself looking to recruit a new salesperson for your organisation. This could be as a result of someone leaving, or a strategic decision to expand the team due to increased market potential, development of new products or a new business site. Some companies also have an ongoing recruitment strategy to enable succession planning, especially if they have a large team, and may always be on the look out for good sales staff, either internally or externally. Whatever the reason, recruitment and selection of new staff can be a costly and time-consuming exercise. If you choose the wrong person to employ, you have the additional concern of putting the situation right and minimising the potential damage it can do.

Salespeople are the lifeblood of any organisation and, without sales being made, nobody else has a job to do. Poor recruitment has far-reaching implications. Think about the cost of first advertising the post, the time involved to sort the applications, prepare for and conduct interviews, offer the position and undertake the induction training. Then consider the salary and benefits you provide, the time during which the new recruit is not generating business and so on. The costs soon mount up! A recent study estimated that somewhere in the region of £16,000 is not an uncommon figure if you choose the wrong applicant!

Add to this the potential damage that recruiting the wrong staff can do to your existing business, to the morale of the existing team, as well as to the reputation of the company, let alone the cost of the time lost when new business was not being generated.

You must exercise due care in adhering to employment legislation: matters such as Equal Opportunities and best practice. You could have a real problem on your hands if it is not handled correctly. Make sure that you are totally up to date and aware of such requirements before you embark on a recruitment campaign.

## Prepare the groundwork

How can you minimise this potential risk and make sure that you manage the process in a thorough, professional way, which is likely to result in the best possible outcome?

First of all, ask yourself the question, 'Do we need to employ someone new?' Quite often we make a knee-jerk reaction to losing a salesperson and want to get a replacement as soon as possible. Consider the following alternative options:

- Does the business need to replace this person?
- Perhaps the area covered is not profitable or business demands are falling?
- Do we have any existing staff who are suitable for this role and we can promote from within?
- Could the workload be shared out amongst the existing team?
- Would reorganising the territories be a good strategic decision?
- How does this fit in with our strategic plan?

*Job description*

If you do decide that a salesperson is needed, the first step is to design a job description, or at least review the existing one for any changes. The job description should spell out very clearly what the job involves and state the key responsibilities of the role, tasks and activities to be undertaken, as well as the overall objective.

For example, specify whether the job holder is responsible for generating only new business, a mixture of new and development, or simply developing existing accounts. Be explicit about the products and services they will be selling, the territory to cover and desired performance outcomes. It is no good having a job description that simply reads: 'Generate more business for the company'.

You need to state the job title, summarise the job purpose and outline the key performance areas you would expect the new recruit to fulfil. For example:

| | |
|---|---|
| Sales Executive | To generate new and to develop existing profitable business in the Cheshire area |

- Win business in line with business objectives
- Develop existing accounts, year on year
- Respond to opportunities to tender for contracts
- Provide after-sales support to new clients for 3 months
- Obtain, analyse and record market information
- Prepare and submit a monthly sales report as per guidelines

For the person specification, do not waste time trying to find someone who does not exist! This document should clearly outline what skills, qualifications, knowledge, experience and background the most suitable individual would have, as well as an idea of the attributes and personality that you feel would be most successful. Make sure that you are not looking for the impossible; be realistic in your aspirations.

## Case study

An organisation is looking for a new salesperson for the Midlands. In their specification they stated that:

> Must have previous advertising sales experience, be educated to degree level (relevant business degree), have at least 3–5 years' experience and be generating in excess of £50,000 per quarter. Ideal candidate would be conversant with the automotive industry, should have experience on working for an automotive manufacturer and have experience of the same geographical area. Salary of £12,000 p.a.

How many applicants do you think met the criteria?

Draw up a list that prioritises your needs, and ensure that you are specific about the essential attributes (i.e. they must have) and those that are desirable (i.e. it would be beneficial if they had). Once you have agreed this, perhaps by discussing it with your line manager, stick to it. Do not fall into the trap of bending the rules if you find someone who is almost what you want, which can happen if we are anxious to hire someone quickly.

The job description and person specification deserve some time and effort to get right. They will prove valuable in preparing for the interview, drawing up an induction plan, ongoing training and development, as well as in performance management once the candidate is in the post. You should also make sure that these documents do not contravene current employment legislation and, again, take advice from someone who is suitably qualified and experienced in this area, if you are not. Remember, you have an obligation both to the business, and by law, to employ the most suitable applicant for the position, regardless of their gender, ethnicity and any disability they may have and so on. It makes good business sense, you will agree, to get the best person for the job, and to make sure that you are conducting yourself in the most professional way.

*Legal considerations*

Briefly, employment law requires that you do not discriminate against any applicant, directly or indirectly, either in your requirements, advertisement, expectations or treatment of them. This book does not provide an in-depth explanation of this field, but you should be aware of The Sex Discrimination Act, The Race Relations Act, and The Disability Discrimination Act, as well as the need to apply a fair and equitable recruitment process. The term 'Best Practice' is often heard, and best practice guidelines, if followed, will help you to apply this to your case. Further information about employment law in the recruitment process can be found in Hodder & Stoughton's publication *Know Your Employment Rights in a week.*

## What to do next?

Do not make the mistake of thinking that you can achieve the best results in a short period of time. You need to allow time to advertise, sift, interview, select and make the offer. Moreover, you have to take into account the period of notice an individual may have to work with their current employer. Make sure your ideal start date for the new recruit is realistic, and that this date also fits in with other business demands.

Check that you will be available to support the new person when they first start and that their induction can be carried out effectively. Ascertain that your time-scale does not influence your decision. Do not choose someone who may be unsuitable just to meet that target! It is tempting to hire the first 'suitable' person that comes along if a business territory is not being covered at the moment, but a rash decision to keep business coming in now can be a costly and troublesome problem in the long term. Recruit in haste, repent at length!

## Advertising the vacancy

Once you have agreed the job description and person specification, you need to consider how you might market the vacancy. Where are salespeople most likely to learn about your vacancy? You should advertise the position internally to current staff whenever possible, in order to offer them the opportunity for promotion or development, but how will you make external applicants aware of the vacancy?

One route you might take is to advertise in a publication, whether a newspaper or industry magazine, or alternatively on the internet, considering your target audience and where they are most likely to see it. Another avenue may be to place the vacancy with a reputable recruitment agency; some specialise in sales positions, and others are more industry-specific. A cost is involved whichever route you take and you must weigh up the pros and cons of each before you proceed.

You should think about the most appropriate way to conduct the screening stage and decide on the most suitable. For example, telephone interviews might be a good choice because with salespeople one of your criteria will be their ability to communicate verbally. Prepare a few questions in advance that will allow you to quickly assess their suitability. From here you can draw up a short-list of people to invite for interview – six to eight is a manageable number – at a time that is mutually convenient.

However, you may prefer to receive written applications directly, in order to assess the candidates' ability to write a persuasive letter. Constantly think about the attributes you would expect a good salesperson to have, and apply this thinking throughout the process.

Some recruitment agencies will take care of this initial stage for you, even advertising the role, sifting through applicants and so on. Nonetheless, you must ensure that they are clear about your criteria and that they do not waste your time forwarding unsuitable applicants.

## Interviews

While the position is marketed, you need to start preparing for the interviews themselves. The crucial first step is to recognise whether you have the skills to conduct an interview. Do not be drawn into thinking that interviews are just about having a quick chat to see if candidates are suitable. You need a structure and some well-thought out probing questions. This will allow you to judge suitability quickly. This is especially important with salespeople. If they are any good in sales, they will be able to build a convincing and persuasive argument, which you need to have the skills to thoroughly check out. Any good salesperson should be able to communicate well and portray themselves in a good light, therefore, well-planned probing questions are a must!

Example questions could include:

- Explain to me your strategy for winning new business
- Give me an example of a new account that you have won recently, which required persistence
- Tell me about how you handled a negotiation with a large contract

It is fair to say that past performance is a good indicator of future expectations – do not employ someone and think: 'It's OK, I can change them'. Chances are, you can't.

You also need to have the skills to set the candidate at ease and to build rapport. Listen to the answers and avoid the temptation to butt in or ask leading questions to get the answer you want. In this vein, you also need to remain objective and unbiased.

To achieve objectivity, a second opinion should always be invited. Perhaps ask the sales director or another relevant member of staff who will have an interest in the new recruit. Just because someone is a member of the same golf club, their children go to the same school as yours, or they share your sense of humour and you like them, does not mean they are the best person for the job! Involving someone else in the recruitment process will help to alleviate potential bias, that often we may not realise we have. Compare applicants to your criteria and not to each other. Do not hurry to hire someone and employ 'the best of a bad bunch', rather than holding out and finding the best person for the job.

The following points serve as a good check-list to apply a systematic and fair procedure:

- Who will conduct the interviews and what will the format be?
- When will you conduct the interviews?
- Make sure that each interview time allows for a thorough discussion to check the candidate's suitability, as well as giving you some breathing space before the next candidate to gather your thoughts and make any notes, and take a comfort break!
- Where will you hold the interviews? Choose somewhere that offers privacy, is quiet, has an area where applicants can wait separately from the interview room, and has easy access for all applicants.
- Prepare a series of good questions that allow you to fully check the candidate's suitability – bear in mind the benefit of open-ended questions to elicit information.

- You might want to ask situational or competence-based questions. Here you ask the applicant to describe to you what they might do if *x* was to happen and how they might handle *y* situation. Take advice on preparing suitable questions if you have no previous experience of this, in order to make the most of the opportunity.
- Your questions should be based on the job description and person specification that you have prepared, to ensure that they are relevant and purposeful.
- Be clear about what you are hoping to find out from your questions – and what the answer would ideally be, again referring back to the job description and person specification.
- Good salespeople should be able to sell themselves well. Make sure their sales pitch is not misleading or flawed.
- Ask all applicants the *same* questions to avoid any risk of bias. Keep brief notes of their responses in case you need to refer back to them. Retain this information on file after the recruitment process, in case your decision is challenged.
- Draw up a decision matrix that you can refer to immediately after the interview. This should draw upon your original person specification and be fair and valid. You might want to put a weighting value on each criteria. This matrix should be completed at the end of each interview and can be used as an objective approach, giving a 'score' for each applicant against your criteria.

- Prepare an agenda for the interview – introduce yourself and relax the interviewee, then include an introduction of the company, outline the role, question to find out about the candidate, and offer the candidate opportunities to ask any questions they have. Conclude by agreeing the next stage and stick to it.

You may also consider the following:

- Would it be appropriate to arrange an assessment centre, where candidates complete a series of exercises, allowing you to check their competence and attitude and perhaps see how they interact with others?
- Is it relevant to have a psychometric profiling or personality profiling exercise as part of the selection process? Make sure the test you use is valid and reliable and that person who will administer the test is suitably qualified, licensed and able to interpret information accurately and without bias. Tools exist that are specifically aimed at salespeople.
- Consider how you will give feedback to applicants. If you arrange assessments and profiling, it is only fair that they receive feedback. Remember, your company's image, reputation and legal standing is at stake here and therefore this needs to be handled well.
- What resources do you need for the interviews, for example, company brochure, marketing information etc. You may also want to use a Polaroid camera to take a snapshot of each applicant, so that you can remember them clearly afterwards.

A recruitment exercise needs to be handled professionally and the timing needs to be right. Do not keep people hanging around for a decision. Acknowledge all applications and write to everyone interviewed as soon as possible after you have made your choice. Good salespeople are rarely on the market for long! Your organisation needs to be seen to be professional and courteous, even to unsuccessful candidates. Remember to keep records and notes on file.

An interview is a two-way process. As well as an opportunity for you to find out about the candidate, it is also for them to decide if they want to work for you. Sell your company, but do not build expectations that might not be met – otherwise you will be recruiting again when the dissatisfied person leaves.

## Summary

Recruitment can be a minefield if you are unaware of the pitfalls. You can see now why it is also a time-consuming and costly exercise if done right, and an absolute catastrophe if handled badly!

- How can you develop your own skills and knowledge further in this area?

Hopefully, after the interviews, you will be able to select a suitable applicant. You need to make sure that a letter is sent to the applicant confirming your offer, stating that it is subject to obtaining satisfactory references, and outlining the information they need to have. Remember to take up references once the conditional offer has been accepted – be thorough in this. You do not want to find that you are employing a salesperson who is currently being disciplined for fraud. Confirm a start date and make sure you have planned and prepared adequately for it.

A letter should be sent to the new recruit detailing the role and the minimum amount of information that is required by law to form their contract. Again, make sure that whoever is responsible for this is suitably qualified and experienced. A duplicate should be sent to allow the candidate to sign and return for your records. Matters such as salary, commission, bonus schemes and company car allowance need to be made explicit from the outset.

So, a new member of your team is soon to join you. Refer back to Thursday's performance management section, and get it right from day one!

# Motivation and reward

Frequently, when you mention the subject of motivation to many managers, they liken the theory to 'carrot and stick'. Now carrots and sticks might work if you are motivating a donkey, but even the animal trainers have long since recognised reward and praise works far better than punishment! However, there are still some managers who believe the autocratic, dictatorial 'If you achieve target, you can keep your job, and if you don't then we'll fire you!' approach is good enough. Think how motivated that would make you feel.

- How do you currently motivate your team?
- Do you realise the impact that your competence and leadership style has on motivating your team?

Your role and responsibility as the sales manager is about much more than your competence and skill in selling, as we have already seen on Sunday. When deliberating how to motivate others, your management and leadership style are of paramount importance. Remind yourself of the qualities and characteristics of a good manager and you will probably recognise that these are the qualities and characteristics that also lead a motivated team.

Are you motivated yourself? It is often said that if you are not motivated, you cannot motivate others.

- Do you demonstrate commitment to the job and the team, have a positive attitude, a desire to succeed, and give credit and acknowledge others' success?
- Do you admit mistakes and learn from them, involve the team in solving problems, making decisions, discussing and agreeing targets and strategies?
- Do you take control when it is needed, when others are looking to you to take the lead?
- Do you take a pride in your appearance, standards of work and time-keeping?
- Are you keen to develop your own skills, as well as those of others around you?
- Are you fair, consistent, honest and open?
- Do you encourage and support others, and support them by identifying where things could be even better?
- Do you foster a good team atmosphere and encourage your team to support each other?
- Do you know your team well, and understand the different personalities, likes and dislikes and what makes them tick?
- Are you good at spotting the team's development needs and helping them to improve?

- Do you appraise your people and their performance regularly?
- Have you recruited the right people for the team?
- Have you given them the right resources and support to achieve the SMART goals and targets you have discussed and agreed?

If you can honestly answer 'Yes' to these questions, without faltering, then the chances are that your team is motivated. You give the team what it needs to feel good about itself, feel supported and encouraged, feel valued and recognised, and the team has the opportunity to succeed and be rewarded accordingly. If, however, there are questions you cannot answer with a definite 'Yes', consider what you need to do about you, before you worry about them! Lead by example.

## How to motivate

Motivation is not something that comes in a bottle, which you can regularly hand out to your team – it goes far deeper than that. Motivation depends on your ability as a manager to provide all the things that your team needs from you, from the organisation and from the job the team is employed to perform. You need to make sure that the factors that fire the team up and make it hungry for business are plentiful, and that where possible, you eliminate or at least reduce factors that drag the team down and take away their enthusiasm for success.

Sounds easy enough, but where people are concerned, nothing is ever that simple. What may make one salesperson full of enthusiasm and energy and motivated to keep going, may not have the same effect on the others. Knowing your team and what it is that makes it tick is paramount.

Often, with salespeople, organisations feel that the best way to motivate them to achieve more is to reward them financially for doing so. Financial incentives do not always lead to increased motivation and increased business. Surprised? Read on.

## Case study

A team of salespeople were all offered a financial incentive to increase business over the quarter. They were each set personal targets for revenue, and anything over that would lead to a 5 per cent commission payment, which represented quite a large sum of money. One individual made a positive decision not to strive for the target she had been set. She was more than capable of doing it, but had calculated that, with the increased bonus payment, her annual earnings would be in the higher tax bracket, and financially the effort was not justified by the reward. Another individual was also uninterested in the extra effort required for the higher earnings – financially he did not need to work, his partner's income was more than sufficient for their needs, and he worked for the satisfaction of having a career – money was not a motivator for him. A third individual did not believe it was realistic to achieve the target because her territory was saturated and she did not believe there was further potential within her current area. She decided that it was not worth the effort as the target was out of her reach.

This situation gives us a clear insight into the most important factor to consider when seeking to motivate others – we need to be clear on what will make the difference. Not everyone is motivated by the same thing and, in fact, for some people, such incentives make absolutely no difference!

## Theories and practice

Much has been written about motivation. Many theories exist that attempt to explain what motivates people. However, we are not too concerned here with the theories, but more with the practicalities of having a highly motivated and successful sales team. You will begin to see that a great deal of what we have discussed previously contributes to how motivated your team is.

On Monday we talked about setting goals and being clear about whether people feel they can achieve them. Vroom's Expectancy theory clearly outlines that people need to want to achieve it (their level of desire), and to feel that they *can* (level of expectancy).

The case study above also highlights the need to understand another theory of motivation that has stood the test of time, Maslow's hierarchy of needs. Abraham Maslow concluded that, as human beings, we have needs that we seek to satisfy. Once one of those needs has been met, we do not look for more of the same, but move on to a higher level. The first level addresses basic physiological needs – warmth, shelter, food and water. We can achieve this through earning a salary that meets these wants. Once we have enough to satisfy this need, we do not necessarily seek more of it, but rather move on to the next level of security. Matters such as job security, a pension scheme, medical insurance perhaps become more attractive. For example, a job with an organisation that is more secure, rather than a job that pays a higher salary, but where there is a constant threat of redundancy. Once we feel that this need has been satisfied, Maslow concluded that we move on to the next – our social needs. A feeling of belonging, friendly and helpful colleagues, a good team atmosphere. Then on to a higher level of self-esteem – possibly met through recognition and praise, additional responsibility, promotion and a higher grade car that promotes our self-image. The ultimate level is self-actualisation – some argue we can never reach this level, but it could involve personal development through jobs that are fulfilling, interesting and that require full use of our capabilities and yet there is scope for further challenge and development. Maybe a salesperson earns enough money to satisfy their needs, and so the opportunity of more will not motivate them. What can you do as their manager to make sure that whatever it is that does motivate them to get out of bed in a morning and do their best is there?

One thing that is certain is that as we grow older and move through life, our priorities change. What was once our primary motivator, is now taken over by something else. Consider the school leaver looking for cash in his back pocket to maintain his social life compared to the married man with children who would prefer less time away from home, rather than the extra money this pays? There are no rules that say, 'At this age/ time in their life people want . . .' – the rule is, we are all different!

- Do you know what the differences are in your team?
- How do you currently cater for those differences in motivating them?

## Incentives and rewards

As we can now see, unlike the belief held by many organisations, financial reward is not always appropriate, and not purely for the reasons identified in our case study. It has been known for financial targets and rewards to become expected; people see them as their entitlement.

Another organisation introduced a bonus scheme for its sales team. They enjoyed the higher earnings that it gave them, but after a while the organisation found the scheme was costing them money – it was not self-financing. The cost of managing and financing the scheme outweighed the value of the increased business. The scheme was withdrawn. The sales team were absolutely horrified – they now considered it their right, their entitlement, to earn such a bonus. They became dissatisfied, morale was low and many chose to leave.

Another company chose to reward its high achievers with a higher grade of company car. When the staff did not achieve their target, what would they do? Downgrade the car to a basic model? People now saw the executive model as their entitlement. Those who continued to meet and exceed target, no longer felt rewarded or motivated because they had reached the highest grade of car available in that range. Short of giving them a high performance, expensive sports car or private helicopter, the reward could not be increased further. They already had the optimum.

- Incentives and rewards can eventually be seen as entitlement; how can you keep increasing the reward to match motivation and achievement?
- Once you have achieved the maximum, what incentive is there to work harder for nothing more?

Another important factor to consider about any commission or incentive scheme, is that the 'ideal' scheme is often impossible to achieve. It can be very difficult to design a reward scheme that is fair and consistent.

- Should support staff who help the sales team also share in the incentive scheme?
- How can you design a system that is self-financing: i.e. that does not cost the company?
- What sort of scheme can you have that is easy to manage, monitor and recognises achievement?

There is little point in having a scheme in place, which is a burden to in administer. If you have to spend a couple of days each month tallying figures, calculating percentages and increased profit margins, can you really say the scheme is worthwhile? The scheme should recognise and reward what is desirable and should be derived from your strategy. It should be relatively transparent so that progress can be easily monitored and, moreover, it should really motivate the team. Now you can see why the ideal scheme is hard to come by!

Furthermore, consider if you use rewards or prizes to motivate. An example might be the reward of a free weekend in a holiday resort or some other equivalent, for the highest achiever. Depending on the measurement, this may unfairly disadvantage those with a saturated territory where there is not the same scope for development of business. It may also demotivate others if one salesperson is seen to take an early lead because of a good 'win'. If one person looks as though they might come in second, by a small margin only, what incentive is there for them to be motivated and continue? They are not going to win, and nor are the others who are also only a whisker behind them.

A different approach is where everyone that achieves, wins. When you cross the line of the London Marathon, you get a medal and recognition that you went the distance. Your motivation and desire is fuelled by the fact that you have finished – you have accomplished something. You never expected to come first, but you kept going, even long after the first hundred had finished hours ahead of you, because there was still something in it for you. Perhaps your scheme would work better if there was a sense of achievement and recognition for everyone who passed the post – not just the one athlete with different personal circumstances who led from the starting line?

Then again, there are people who would never want to run the London Marathon – maybe the effort required does not justify the potential reward, perhaps it does not appeal to them or the accomplishment does not serve to meet any of their personal needs? They would be more motivated by organising sponsorship for others to raise money for charity – satisfaction coming from raising the money and contributing in this way. Whether your team wants to run the marathon, or whether other involvement fires them up further, you need to know what it takes to motivate them.

The other thing to bear in mind about money is that we recognise that people sometimes change jobs for less money. Hard for some people to understand, but if that job gives the individual something else that they crave, we can see how Maslow's hierarchy has remained credible. They might seek another position, which although it pays less, gives them more time to spend with their family. It may give them the challenge they need, the recognition they desire, the additional responsibility they feel they deserve. The new organisation may offer better prospects for promotion, increased development and learning opportunities, a greater satisfaction in what they do. It may enable them to satisfy their ego by giving them status, a title, or pride in working for a high value name.

Money is not everything to everyone. What is it that motivates you? Not running the marathon yourself, but supporting others and being proud of their achievement? A good sales manager will get their 'feel good factor' from being the support in the marathon, not from wearing the medal themself.

One of the main motivators for many is the recognition and appreciation of their work by their manager. Recognise and support the achievement of others, take pride in their achievement, and the contribution you made to that, and give them the resources they need to cross that finishing line – regardless of whether they are first, second or twentieth! By the way, remember to say 'Thanks for doing such a great job!' So many managers miss the importance of this, and what's more, it is free and easy to do! Just watch people smile, grow in height and have a bounce in their step – assuming you are genuine, of course.

- Are you motivating and encouraging your team?
- What else can you do to help motivate them?

## More motivation

Sales meetings should be events that your team look forward to, participate in, contribute to, and come away from buzzing with a desire to go out there and win business. Are you making the most of sales meetings as motivational moments? Are they properly planned, everyone involved, worthwhile and useful and used to recognise and reward, rather than berate and punish? Perhaps consider devoting a part of the meeting to help the team to consider 'difficult questions' they might get asked on a call, awkward objections that keep cropping up or ways to handle difficult clients who 'play games'. Use the meetings as opportunities to develop the salespeople's skills and knowledge, a chance to learn, spend time with others, in a positive environment where people are encouraged and valued. Make sure your team look forward to the meetings and leave them on a high and ready to go sell.

You could offer your team an opening to develop skills in other areas of the organisation, which may indeed help to increase their sales effectiveness. However, at the same time it will give them more variety, personal development and opportunities for career progression at a later date.

Perhaps sponsor the team to complete a business-related qualification, that will not only satisfy their own sense of achievement, but also add to the success of the organisation. You could introduce a flexitime system, which enables those who enjoy time with their family, in pursuit of a hobby or pastime or travelling, to satisfy their personal needs.

While you contemplate ways to motivate, analyse whether any of your behaviours and practices serve to demotivate.

- Do you put unnecessary obstacles in the way of your team that might dilute motivation?
- Are there cumbersome administrative systems or procedures that take more time and hassle to complete and so outweigh the benefits of having them?
- Do the team have to work in an environment that is not conducive to good team relations?
- Is it an environment which does not look after their basic health and safety needs?
- Do the team have to share work space, and are remote and alienated from colleagues, so that a sense of true belonging and value are never forthcoming?
- Are the team kept in the dark and not treated as important and valued individuals, with unclear and infrequent communication?

## Summary

A highly skilled and motivated team is the best sort of team a sales manager could wish for. Before you begin to examine your team and their effort, behaviour and contribution, you need to examine yourself.

- Do you have the necessary skills?
- Are you competent as a manager?

A good salesperson does not always make a good manager. In addition to focusing on having a high performing team, ask yourself the question – 'Do my team have a high performing manager?' It is not an easy job, but sales management can be an extremely rewarding and challenging one. How competent the manager is can be a crucial factor in motivating and inspiring others to succeed – best of luck!

Andrea Newton can be contacted through her website www.abdtraining.co.uk